"<u>Young Knowledge</u>"

My Advice to Young Men

Insights on how to change your way of thinking and living

Written by,
Andre Guzman

Dedicated to all of my young men locked up. Everything is going to be okay.

What you are about to read:

Foresight- My Young Men, you are Young Kings! A King conducts himself with high standards, morals, values and ethics, and is a productive member of society.

How to Dress- Always be presentable.

What to watch on TV- Be careful, everything isn't what it seems.

Way of speech- We've gone away from our articulateness.

Friends or Associates- Watch who you surround yourself with.

Music- Negative consumption in the mind is a huge hindrance to the growth you need to develop.

Drugs- You need to focus and stay strong psychologically.

Staying Positive- Hard to do at times, but it's a must do thing.

Being Selfless- It's not just about you anymore.

In Closing- I want you to be the King that you are!

Glossary- Lets expand our vocabulary together.

My life now- My success from CHANGE.

"About myself"

My name is Andre Guzman; my guys call me "Professor Andre." Ha-ha I love you guys. I'm a twenty four year old father with two kids. My birthday is August tenth, nineteen eighty nine, which makes me a Leo. I was born and raised in Merced California, "The Central Valley" or the "Country" of California, people like to say because we have lots of farms. It's an agricultural town that's growing.

I grew up in a neighborhood called the "Meadows" on Meadows Avenue located on the north side of town. I come from a family of gang members, so growing up in that particular setting, it was everywhere I went, especially right by my house, and there were shootings and fights every other day.

But I still stayed in school, one, because I love to learn and two, because Uncle James would beat me up if I didn't. Uncle James is a five foot two Giant who's a Golden Glove. I didn't want to mess with him and still don't, and I'm six foot three. But he's a good man that taught me a lot. I learned how to work and become a man listening to Uncle James. However, I still went against the teachings because I wanted to be well known in the streets, which caused me to go to juvenile hall and in and out of jail constantly, violation after violation.

I wasn't able to see my junior BabyDre born. I wasn't there for my daughter's gymnastics. Because of the lifestyle I chose to live, since I was eighteen I've only been home two and a half years, two of those years being spent in a program called, Delancey street foundation. When I was twenty-two years old I was facing fifteen years in the penitentiary for violating probation again for the third time, I was caught being around some people I wasn't supposed to be around and there was guns at the particular location as well. At the time I thought I was done, but I was tired and wanted to change really bad, so I wrote the judge, my public defender, the district attorney, Delancey Street Foundation and the supervisor of probation asking for a chance at life and to be able to change who I was. So that way I could be in my children's lives and give back to the community what I owe.

I have always had a feeling that I was supposed to be doing something different in life, something greater than myself that the youth in my community need. I wanted to dedicate my life to helping them. That's how I changed my life, by putting somebody else before myself. That's what I've learned through due time and that is what I practiced on a daily basis in The Delancey Street Foundation program: You put others before yourself and everything else will fall in place.

My favorite quote by the famous motivational speaker and author, Zig Ziglar is, *"You can have everything in life you want if you will just help enough people get what they want."* He spoke in the business aspect, but I think we can correlate that with everything. The difference about me is I'm not worried about going to some top. I'm just giving back. I feel it's my duty and my calling: to dedicate my life to helping people, so that way they're not subjected to the same things that I was.

"Foresight"

I feel it's a necessity for all young men to conduct themselves in a professional, high standard manner. Whether incarcerated or free from cell doors, it's a must-do thing. If you want to be successful later on in life, you need to conduct yourself in a certain type of fashion now. Essentially you will become what you want to become. In psychology it's called, "acting as if." You need to act as if you already are, in order to become. But not just to become, but because that'll be a huge part needed to be practiced in changing your life. It all starts with how you look, conduct yourself, to your way of speaking.

And first it starts with how you think. The mentality has to be totally different immediately. It'll take some time, but that's why I've written these insights, to teach how. And I believe that if you practice these insights, not only will you stay out of trouble, but you will be that example in the community that young men will look up to and emulate in a positive way.

You'll be that guy that your family will be proud of. Plus you will be one less statistic away from those walls that a young smart, likeable, successful young man that you are shouldn't be subjected to. You will be free, and a productive member of society.

It's easy to be that negative individual causing mischief so the district attorney wants to incarcerate you and throw away the key. All of the things that happen to us are because we subject ourselves to the situations in the first place. To have to go through those circumstances in general is not cool. Really, that's not who you are; that's not who you were created to be and do.

You have the potential and inner capabilities that need to be tested to the fullest capacity, and it all starts with you. It doesn't matter if you have a record or one hundred tattoos on your body. Even though presentation is everything, based on perception, really it's all in your approach and how you conduct yourself. This pertains to getting a job as well.

That's why I felt I should offer these insights. From one young man to another, we build each other up, NOT knock each other down. I know how it feels to think that there's no other way than what you might be going through at the moment. I know because I've been there, in and out of jail, gangs, sold drugs and everything else that came with that negative lifestyle. I want you to understand my main objective. "A real leader makes those who follow him leaders as well". That's not just my duty but yours as well. We have a responsibility to make a difference in the community, to bring our lost men back into the correct and right state of mind, not only for yourself but so that others will not be subjected to incarceration or drugs.

So enjoy and actually make an effort to change. Your future is Greater than what you can imagine. You just have to BELIEVE in yourself. If you don't, I do, that's why I've written these insights. Just for you-- Gentlemen less fortunate who may think there's only one way to live. I'm here to let you know there's a better way and I want you to be successful because you are a King.

"Way of Speech "

Coming from where we come from such as the projects, juvenile halls, youth authorities and the penitentiary, you develop a vocabulary only comprehensible to those secular types of individuals. This is not good at all! And it's insignificant in the real world. Changing it immediately will be hard, I understand that, but it's something that must be done consciously if you want to change.

When you're going to a job interview, how are you going to speak? If you walk in with your pants sagging and speaking Ebonics, you're not getting the job. You walk in with the appropriate attire and speaking in a sophisticated manner, and then you just might get that chance.

Now you're already stereotyped. Maybe it's because you have tattoos or a record. As straight forward as that may sound, it's the truth. Be aware that whatever it is that makes you stand out gets you stereotyped. So in general you want that first impression of yours to be positive all around for anybody, and not just impressing that hiring manager with how you carry yourself. Their pre-conceived notion just went out the door and not just changed towards you but to other young gentleman with the same type of stereotypes.

So sometimes just based on the impression you make, you can be changing someone else at the same time. Their perspective just did a total one eighty. You made a difference and that's what I meant in the foresight about being that example. It doesn't mean that you're a "square" because you're elevating your speech. I've gotten called those things as well. But you know what? In reality there's no such thing as talking like a "square." Wouldn't you rather sound highly sophisticated like you've got some sense rather than sounding ignorant like you have no sense at all?

Read books! I want to emphasize reading a lot. Retaining information is imperative. Technology is constantly advancing. The human mind is consistently advancing and we should be keeping up. When you come across a word you don't understand, write it down, look it up in the dictionary, study it and implement it into your everyday vocabulary. This leads me to the dictionary. I used to scan through the dictionary and if I liked certain words then I would memorize them and speak to my friends about them until naturally they were utilized in my everyday speech.

Malcolm X, during his seven out of a ten-year sentence, read voraciously and hand copied the entire dictionary. This made his vocabulary substantial. You can do the same, or more. It just takes practice.

"Friends"

You must change who you surround yourself with. A friend that has your best interest is going to try to do nothing but help you excel in life. If I make it then you make it, in the positive aspect. A friend isn't going to get you subjected to drugs, violence or incarceration.

I know from experience that the only person that's going to be there for you in the end is your family, the ones that matter. One of my favorite quotes is by Dr. Seuss, *"Be who you are and say what you feel because those who mind don't matter and those who matter don't mind."* That negative secular group of so-called friends will have you in jail, without a job, with no girlfriend. I can guarantee that; I can do nothing but be honest with you. That's why these insights are important. I want you to look at things from a whole different perspective. I want you to succeed in life, make it as far away from the system that you possibly can by being a good person and helping others do the same.

I care and wish to hear from all of my readers. I'm your friend for life, and with me I can promise that not only will I not lead you astray, but I will be there for you. When needed I can be reached anytime. I'm here for you. And that's how every friend should be.

Furthermore, your friends play a huge part in whether you succeed or fail because you are who you surround yourself with. You hang around ten gang members who commit crimes and do drugs, then slowly but surely you'll be committing crimes and doing drugs as well. That's what you'll become. If you hang around ten successful, positive business men who invest, build and make huge impacts in the community, well guess what, that is what you will essentially become. Self explanatory, right?

Get with one of your friends who are also tired of the way of life that's leading you both nowhere. Get with someone who is also trying to change his way of thinking and living and study these insights together, practice, and review with each other the insights accumulated. Make plans, goals, discuss change and grow together. Real friends peer pressure each other to be the best of themselves, not the worst. So remember that.

"Music"

We have these mainstream artists sending negative messages which influence our youth to do some crazy things. It's the truth. I remember listening to a song by two chains, totally vulgar! And I know for a fact that he's not practicing what he's preaching because I'm from the streets and one thing that we didn't do was talk about the things that we did because we did what we had to do to survive. And now these mainstream artists have people who grew up in marginalized communities depicted as robbers, drug dealers, pimps and thugs, when in reality that's not everything that we are about.

We are Good people who are trying to make it in life everywhere. Just because there's a lot of people in poverty and/or committing crimes doesn't necessarily mean that we are all bad people. That's where the game is twisted and it must be fixed. We as a people must not fall into that particular influence and become manipulated by that nonsense. We are better than that.. So you know just like I know that it's fake and it's not right to have such an influence.

Now I'm just using that one artist as an example but the amount of people involved with this is substantial, and it's upsetting and scary. And they are rich because of it. In our communities there are actual acts of violence because of these specific messages being sent through music. Right, it's totally a problem that's affecting how people view us as a whole. That's why I've created my own album as well, full of positive, real life issues. It's inspirational, and motivational in a positive way with real lyrics that'll make you think about getting out there to make a positive impact in the hood yourself and to just make people feel good, because not everyone's happy. Music is supposed to be one of those outlets to fall on when stressed or upset. Especially in the hood!

We grow up listening to music, rapping and singing as a talent. That was everybody's dream in my neighborhood, to be on M.T.V or B.E.T, Rap city in the basement or on 106th and Park. But why not listen to music that's going to uplift you to do positive things, music that gives you that extra boost to accomplish goals in life or to go help somebody? I'm tired of our troubled youth being viewed as if they're bad people because of how mainstream artists project us to be. Every person that's growing up in a marginalized community is not a gangster, robber, or pimp. Many of us are doing the right thing. And many of us have changed our lives and are now doing the right thing even if we haven't before (using as an example in that aspect).

So, my friends please watch what you listen to. Music has such a strong influence, it makes us feel certain types of ways and depending on what type of mood you're in at the moment, without self discipline and control, the wrong kind of music can influence us to do wrong things. This is what I'm trying so hard to keep you guys away from. Even some r & b is unacceptable because it talks way too much about sex, and I mean WOW! Seriously, that shouldn't be on the forefront of our cerebrums. We should and must be focused on the prize in life, (Success) no matter what.

So yes, music can also be a huge distraction on our mission to success. Be careful what you listen to because not everything is good for you. We want clear minds. Stay away from things that will cloud it.

"What to Watch on T.V."

Now I'm not saying not to watch TV at all, just make sure that what you are watching is educational. We should constantly be learning no matter what. So a lot of programs on TV aren't enlightening or educational. It's the truth.

Now I'm not down-playing or speaking badly about any particular programs, but what I'm saying is use your best judgment. A lot of what's on is just entertainment. Just like these fake rappers on the radio. That's it!

The best way to entertain yourself is with knowledge. You want every minute of the day to be beneficial psychologically. You know about the cause and affect concept: if you think positive, positive things will happen, if you think negative, then of course negative thing will happen. It's all in your head. What you consume psychologically can either be a hindrance or a growth. You don't want those negative vibrations which are totally uncomfortable and not good for the mind; you only want the positive accumulated. We are trying to succeed in life, and anything that could take us away from reaching that goal is a straight distraction.

What I suggest is History channels, Discovery, world news, just anything you can learn something from. Sitting down being glued to a screen anyway is a waste of time in my opinion unless I'm watching something that I can utilize, whether to teach to some troubled youth, my kids, or just to have an intellectual conversation with some friends at a coffee shop or at a meeting talking about our next plan to save the hood. That's why we were created: to help one another. So if what you are accumulating psychologically is a hindrance, then how are you going to be able to help people? Think about it!

I say watch the world news because it's good to know about current events. Those are good conversation starters. Plus you'll hear about positive topics to talk to anybody about. You can converse with anybody on any level in that matter. History channel has so many cool shows that you can learn a variety of information in all aspects. Watching History is like reading books in my opinion. "H2" is actually my favorite. I like watching "Bleeped up brain," "Ancient Aliens" and the "Book of Secrets". These are great shows and you should totally check them out. "Discovery!" as well, I mean who doesn't like animals, right? Plus there's so much to know about living on this beautiful Giant Living Organism we walk upon everyday that we call Earth. There are so many beautiful places all around the globe that we haven't seen or been to physically that can learn about by watching Discovery.

I know you understand what I mean. Its all about learning, and the best way, and the positive way is not only just those channels, but anything that sends messages in a positive way period. If it doesn't, please stay away from it; I want you to stay on point with a focused mindset.

"Stay away from Drugs"

You have the will power to quit! And if you haven't done any, Very well, then you have a Degree of Advantage which you should keep. Doing drugs not only causes dysfunctional thinking, but it makes you extremely vulnerable, and with vulnerability you are easily manipulated. When easily manipulated, then you can easily subject yourself to things that you normally wouldn't do if you were sober.

A lot of people in the world commit crimes under the influence. Let's think about this. When you're sober, you are thinking clearly (of course, right?) and thinking clear;y causes us to make the right decisions. Under the influence causes us to react at an instant because there's no clarity, the drug has taken over your mind and is not allowing you to utilize your consciousness. (This is not good at all!) Many people use the excuse that "marijuana doesn't do anything to you and its good for you!" That's a lie! It decreases your brain cells that you need to think clearly to be able to learn and memorize. Eventually you'll start forgetting small things like where you just put your car keys or cell phone. It's as if you have Alzheimer's at a young age. That's ridiculous and embarrassing.

I know people that I've known since we were children, who are heavy smokers, and I may not be the smartest guy in the world, but I believe my vocabulary is a little extensive. So when I have conversations with them, I have to speak in a language they can understand, because at times they'll ask me "what does that word mean?" or they think that I think, I'm better than they are. Now I love people and I only wish the best for them and would save all the hoods if I could, but I feel bad because many of us are the same age but because of the excessive smoking of marijuana, it has made them slow, literally!

So stay away from it, period. It's not good for your mind. I don't care who says different, it's the truth. Plus it will lead you to other drugs. You will eventually reach a level of tolerance where you are so used to it that you'll search for something different to reach a higher level. Next you're smoking crack, which is intense and very scary.

I hope in my heart that you are receptive to this; it will affect every part of your life. You are so much better than some quick feel good. You are worth way more than an act of ignorance. It's not attractive to sit back laughing at anything, eating substantially like you're starving, and doing absolutely nothing! We want to be productive in life and in order to get somewhere in life in a positive manner, we must stay away from the things that will be a total hindrance to our ways of thinking and will essentially effect our behaviors. Young men who are incarcerated are already depicted as ignorant, so let's break the depiction with intellect.

"How to Dress"

I feel this is very important, especially with our generation and how we feel we have to keep up with the new "trends," so to speak. In reality you don't have to, and you shouldn't. Yes, presentation does have a lot to do with perception as well.

In general, people are more nice and receptive to people who are well dressed. It's the truth, and let me explain why. When I used to be involved in gangs, I dressed for what was appropriate for that specific setting: the all red, because of the color I was representing, the sagging of the jeans, the fitted hat and flashy jewelry, I mean, come on now, that was not attractive or cool at all! And you're not going to see a gang member on the block in a full suit. It just doesn't work like that. The whole street style of dress in general is negative attention and people just don't want to speak with someone looking like a thug. You'll just attract people of the same lifestyle and you don't want that. And I don't care what the new trend is, if it's not business attire or casual, stay away from it.

Grown men should not be dressed like ten year old kids. You have to understand that.

Now there are exceptional settings such as when it's time to relax or a BBQ, sitting at home on your day off from work. Those are pretty much self explanatory, but in public, dress to impress. Now I'm not saying be in a full suit everyday, but slacks, dress shirt, dress shoes, casual at times. Switch it up, but dresss professionally. Every other style in my opinion is being a follower. These fake rappers you see on TV that send negative messages in their music, dress certain types of ways. This influences our young men and women to emulate them in all aspects of life.

Now we have young men sagging at eight years old and young women "twerking" and wearing spandex and shorts that show their private parts like it's the thing to do when its NOT. They see these images and it's automatic. We saw little Wayne sagging and felt we had to because we thought he was cool. Can't you see what I'm saying? We want to be successful in our lives, and part of changing your life is changing how you dress (your image). We are now examples of how to conduct ourselves and your image is very important.

You will always see me well dressed, because I feel good about how I look when I'm dressed up. Put a suit on and go look in the mirror. How do you feel? Go to the mall and hang out with some positive friends and see what type of attention you get. Even see what type of people come talk to you. People will even look at you differently, trust me, this is real! So switch it up because in order to get the proper respect from the correct people, you need to have respect for yourself first and foremost.

Being well dressed displays confidence. You never know who will approach you, you just might meet that new girlfriend or that opportunity to excel in life with some Chief Executive Officer who just might have been looking for somebody to mentor and at the moment, he/she just took an interest in you because you stood out. You never know. Just try it out you'll love who you are becoming.

"Staying Positive"

It's going to be hard but no matter what, this is what you're going to have to do despite any and all circumstances. A lot of times we fail to do this, because something might happen that just might trigger a certain emotion that might make us want to react in a negative manner .But we cannot afford to react in those manners anymore. That's not who you are, what you are or who you are going to be in life, period! With a clear and positive mind we can react in positive ways every time. Of course it takes practice, especially coming from just reacting to now thinking more than twice on how you should respond before you do anything.

This is imperative, but very simple; you do not want to be miserable, right? Nobody does! So to avoid such, you must look at the good in everything and everybody, no matter what, even at those times when you don't feel like you want to. It's just going to make you a better person. That doesn't sound difficult to do, right, especially now that you're going to become a Gentleman, A REAL Gentleman. It's easy.

Everybody has flaws but if that's all we focus on then you'll never receive the lessons or the message you were supposed to learn from that specific person or situation. The only time that we should focus on the flaws in people is when we are helping somebody out. But they have to be open for the constructive criticism as well. So it's a two way street.

My grandma died August fourth, 2012, six days before my birthday. This is a woman who raised me, and I love her so dearly still to this day, I feel that there's something missing in my life, but then at times also I feel her presence. When she died, I had to constantly remind myself that grandma is in a better place with no more suffering. At that particular time there was a lot going on in my life, but at the same time I didn't want to ruin what I had going for myself, over the way that I was feeling when grandma passed away. I had to think about how she would want me to act, and how my kids will look at the circumstance as well as all of the guys I mentor. How would everybody feel, or see me, especially with me teaching ways to be as a young, professional man. I had to really take a look at myself and re-evaluate my whole situation, which at times is the best thing a Gentleman can and should do with every moment. Grandma was very spiritual as well and it took some time with me being in my head, convincing myself that she's in Heaven and that I should continue to do good because that is what she expects for me to do.

So I channeled that energy into a positive and started to focus again, because that's what it's about. That's an example for you of an emotional situation that happened in my life that could have had turned me into some negative and bitter type of guy, which many people become in those types of situations.

What matters is how we respond, overcoming those moments in a positive manner, looking at the good in the situation even when we feel it's an upsetting moment. We develop a higher tolerance for things and start to look at things from a totally different perspective. We get to that point in our lives that after climbing over so many mountains, we just end up turning into better people on the inside.

Next thing you know, good things just start happening for you. That positive energy just keeps coming your way abundantly, and you still remain focused because anything can still happen. And with that right way of thinking, you'll be prepared for it, whatever and whenever. Nothing will affect you in a negative way. That particular energy will just flow past you.

Always remember that negative things are going to happen in life, like we might get our car stolen, lose money, someone we love, a job, or whatever the case may be. That's life! We are only human beings so we are not perfect. Even if we won't have the best of the best lives, be we can control how we react to every circumstance, and the best way to respond is in a positive way.

"Being Selfless"

This is very hard for a lot of us to do. Everything is about me, me and me, when it's not just you, you and you. It's not a good way to think. When all that you're thinking about is yourself, you're setting yourself up for failure. As I write these insights I mainly think about how to convey messages to you, Gentleman, with understanding and as eloquently as possible. That way not only will you understand, but it'll have you thinking in depth, wanting to actually apply what you're reading into your life and be that Change. What I say and write is always about you and for you.

I'm constantly thinking about how I can reach you in a manner where not only do you follow where I'm coming from, but your well being is protected. That way you're not subjected to some of the things that the world offers to keep you suppressed by occupying your mind with frivolous information that takes up space in your mind to keep you away from reality so that you're not focused on what you should be doing. This is done to too many of our troubled youth.

So it helps me in general to help others because I just might be going through something, but when I put others before myself, not only do I forget about what I might be going through in that moment, it also helps me to feel good and better about myself. Gandhi said, *"In order to find yourself is to be in service of others."* This is very important in all aspects.

Look at all of these Great people in our times here in America who put themselves before other people to make a difference. For instance, I like talking about Harriet Tubman because she helped to free over three hundred slaves. I mean it took her about nineteen times running back and fourth to do this, but she did this by herself. Now isn't that amazing? Look at Martin Luther King, look at Malcolm X, and look at Cesar Chavez who created the United Farm Workers. These are just a few, but of course there are so many more. These are just mentioned as examples that were so powerful.

And guess what, young man, we have those same capabilities, it's just all on YOU. What are you going to do right now, not only to change your way of thinking and living, but how are you going to give back to the community?

The community NEEDS your help. Our young men and women are out there dying, trying to make it in these urban communities, waiting for that new person to come through and say "Everything is going to be okay" because I can teach you how! Now that's powerful! But like I said, it's all up to you.

It starts with you changing your way of thinking and then trying to help every person you see down and out, Now I don't mean get out there and give money to every homeless person or to everyone you know needs a couple of dollars for something. No! What I'm saying is give them food for thought, give them knowledge, wisdom and understanding. Give them HOPE. At times that's all we need, that little extra push in life, all from an encouraging, inspiring conversation. I know you can do that, because I have faith in you. And it takes us to be there for our young men in the first place, because they will relate to you. We been through it, we know the struggle, and we know how it feels to be chastised and put on the backburner. But you know what? We've got this! And it all starts by you being selfless, not selfish.

In Closing,

I would like to thank you. I would like to thank you for being that one less young man out of the way. That one less young man that people don't have to say is a trouble maker or a menace to society, when in fact you're none of that. You're a smart, well mannered young Man. Remember that we want people to Respect us, not fear us.

We are already depicted in a certain fashion that has people in fear of us, so let's break that image, by not only being Positive Productive Members of Society but by being examples in the Hood. By being that guy people can come and talk to when they need help or have problems in life, because they trust that our advice will not only help them but give them Hope and Inspiration. You have it in you and I would love to be that Role Model for you as well. You can definitely call on me, anytime of the day and night and ill be there for you.

I will not shun or treat people as if they don't even exist, when they do. I see these Beautiful faces everyday and I smile because I see myself. Practice my advice; put your own twist on it if you want just as long as it's positive and you're doing the Right thing because people need us. There isn't some new prophet that's going to come and save the Hood, it is the Hood that's going to save the Hood. It all starts with us getting involved in our communities and making differences one young man at a time. It is a necessity, and these negative entities have to be removed from our lives and our minds as well.

We have to stay away from the drugs, and we have to stay away from the people who are not trying to do the right thing. We have to change the way that we talk because we are not ignorant. We have to stay away from the music that makes us feel that we have to commit crimes or be some type of way to be popular.

We have to be totally careful about what we watch on TV because we don't want to get hooked on some nonsense that's not going to take us anywhere. And when something happens in life, because at times things don't necessarily go our way, we have to pick ourselves up. We were gifted with resilience naturally. And in those moments our reaction has to be positive no matter what.

Your presentation has to be on point. Forget trying to dress like other people. I remember Steve Harvey saying he invented his clothing line, "Steve Harvey apparel," for young men to dress nice and be presentable, but affordable to us at the Burlington Coat Factory. So all the money you spend on other things to keep up with the trends of society, you can be spending on some clothes that make you look good and feel good in a professional way. Because you are a Professional and you are a Gentleman.

And yes you have to be selfless. It's not about you anymore, it's about that next young man who thinks he's the next one to get shipped to the cell doors, you follow me? We need Leaders for our fellow men, but it all starts with us being the Teachers. And we cannot give up, even though we might not see any changes in the world, what we can do is focus on the ones we see in front of us. Let's change our way of thinking and living today because we are Kings.

My Young Men, you are Young Kings! A King conducts himself with high standards, morals, values and ethics, And is a productive member of society.

Glossary

Accumulated- gather together or acquire an increasing number or quantity of.

Activist- An activist is a person who campaigns for some kind of social change. When you participate in a march protesting the closing of a neighborhood library, you're an activist. Someone who's actively involved in a protest or a political or social cause can be called an activist.

Advocate- a person who publicly supports or recommends a particular cause or policy.

Alzheimer's- progressive mental deterioration that can occur in middle or old age, due to generalized degeneration of the brain. It is the most common cause of premature senility.

Cerebrum- the principal and most anterior part of the brain in vertebrates, located in the front area of the skull and consisting of two hemispheres, left and right, separated by a fissure. It is responsible for the integration of complex sensory and neural functions and the initiation and coordination of voluntary activity in the body.

Chastised- rebuke or reprimand severely.

Channeled-direct toward a particular end or object.

Conduct- the manner in which a person behaves, especially on a particular occasion or in a particular context.

Consciousness- the quality or state of awareness, or of being aware of an external object or something within oneself. It has also been defined as: sentience, awareness, subjectivity, the ability to experience or to feel, wakefulness, having a sense of selfhood, and the executive control system of the mind.

Convey- make (an idea, impression, or feeling) known or understandable to someone and/ or communicate (a message or information).

Depiction - the action or result of showing or representing something, especially in art.

Dysfunctional- deviating from the norms of social behavior in a way regarded as bad.

Eloquent- fluent or persuasive in speaking or writing.

Emulate- to be like and/or surpass.

Entities- a thing with distinct and independent existence.

Extensive- covering or affecting a large area.

Exert- apply or bring to bear (a force, influence, or quality).

Foresight- the ability to predict or the action of predicting what will happen or be needed in the future.

Frivolous- not having any serious purpose or value.

Hindrance- a thing that provides resistance, delay, or obstruction to something or someone.

Imperative- of vital importance; crucial.

King- the male ruler of an independent state, especially one who inherits the position by right of birth.

Manipulation- is the skillful handling, controlling or using of something or someone.

Morals- a person's standards of behavior or beliefs concerning what is and is not acceptable for them to do.

Perspective- a particular evaluation or assessment of something or a situation; point-of-view; or the art of drawing solid objects on a two-dimensional surface so as to give the right impression of their height, width, depth, and position in relation to each other when viewed from a particular point.

Receptive- able or willing to receive something, especially signals or stimuli, and/or willing to consider or accept new suggestions and ideas.

Resilience- the capacity to recover quickly from difficulties; toughness

Substantial- of considerable importance, size, or worth.

Tolerance- the ability or willingness to accept or endure something, in particular the existence of opinions or behavior that one does not necessarily agree with.

Values- a person's principles or standards of behavior; one's judgment of what is important in life.

Voraciously- having a very eager approach to an activity

Vulgar- lacking sophistication or good taste; unrefined and/or making explicit and offensive reference to sex or bodily functions; coarse and rude.

Vulnerability- susceptible to physical or emotional attack or harm.

"My Life Now"

When I decided to change my life, I just knew within my heart that through that transition alone one day I would be successful if I just stayed positive. Even inside those walls, as hard as it was for me being away from my family and facing fifteen years in prison, I still managed to have the ability to put my head up high with confidence and motivation. And because of that transition and positive outlook, my whole situation changed and things just started to work out for me.

I'm doing absolutely great. Life is good, because I chose to make positive decisions in my life, and still continue to make those positive choices because technically I'm just like you, against all odds.

Despite what we are against, I still managed to obtain my own house; fortunately my lovely children are in my life. I currently go to college online at the University of Phoenix; I'm going for my bachelor's degree in psychology so I can learn the technical aspects of the brain and how it affects behavior and so forth to be able to utilize those tools to help people.

Because that's what's it's about. Remember it's not about you anymore; it's about helping others overcome their obstacles so they can get out of a current situation a changed person, or just improve in general. Helping people feel good. After I receive my Bachelors degree I will go for my Masters in social work, so I can be even more effective as an advocate in the community.

Currently I work for the Human Services Agency as a special Projects Coordinator for the Leadership for life program. Also I am a facilitator for the All Dads Matter program where we help fathers navigate the systems that impact their families and teach them how to communicate more effectively so they can be an advocate for themselves and for their family. I have so much fun working with the people I do, plus I am so grateful that I have been given the opportunity to be successful.

I want you to understand that change is possible. You should never give up on yourself, even if the world seems as if it has given up on you. Remember whatever energy you choose to exert out to people and/or to the universe, it will come back to you. Being aware of this, then you should remember to exert nothing but positive energy. I'm living proof that change can be done and also that change will lead you to be successful.